Nifty Thrifty Crafts for Kids

Nifty Thrifty

SPACE

Crafts

P.M. Boekhoff

Enslow Elementary

an imprint of

Enslow Publishers, Inc.

40 Industrial Road
Box 398
Berkeley Heights, NJ 07922
USA

http://www.enslow.com

Library of Congress Cataloging-in-Publication Data

Boekhoff, P. M. (Patti Marlene), 1957-
   Nifty thrifty space crafts / P.M. Boekhoff. — 1st ed.
     p. cm. — (Nifty thrifty crafts for kids)
   Includes index.
   ISBN-13: 978-0-7660-2783-1
   ISBN-10: 0-7660-2783-X
   1. Space vehicles—Models—Juvenile literature. 2. Astronomical models—Juvenile literature.
   I. Title. II. Series.
   TL844.B64 2006
   629.47022'8—dc22

                                       2006006690

Printed in the United States of America

10 9 8 7 6 5 4 3 2 1

To Our Readers:
We have done our best to make sure all Internet Addresses in this book were active and appropriate when we went to press. However, the author and the publisher have no control over and assume no liability for the material available on those Internet sites or on other Web sites they may link to. Any comments or suggestions can be sent by e-mail to comments@enslow.com or to the address on the back cover.

Every effort has been made to locate all copyright holders of material used in this book. If any errors or omissions have occurred, corrections will be made in future editions of this book.

Illustration Credits: Crafts prepared by June Ponte; photography by Nicole diMella/Enslow Publishers, Inc.; Hemera Technologies, Inc. 1997-2000, pp. 2, 30, 31, 32; Tom LaBaff, p. 26; NASA, p. 4; NASA, JPL, p. 5.

Cover Illustration: Photography by Nicole diMella/Enslow Publishers, Inc.

Safety Note: Be sure to ask for help from an adult, if needed, to complete these crafts!

Contents

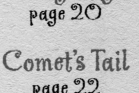

Space!

We are all astronauts flying through space. Earth is our spaceship. Earth spins around like a top as it travels in a big circle, called an orbit, around the Sun. Earth is flying through space at about 93,000 miles per hour and spinning at the same time. Even someone who is sitting very still is flying and spinning through space on Earth.

Everything moves in space. Small planets circle around bigger planets. The Moon is a natural satellite that circles around the Earth. Some planets have many moons, and some have rings of

Space Shuttle *Atlantis* takes off. The astronauts on board were studying the planet Earth.

flying rocks circling around them. These flying rocks are ice and dust particles.

Comets are icy gassy rocks that are pulled toward the Sun. The Sun burns off the gas and ice, which makes a long tail of light.

Planets and many moons circle around the Sun. They are part of the Solar System. Solar means Sun. Each planet makes its orbit around the Sun. The Earth is the third planet from the Sun.

The Sun is a star, like the stars we see at night. Some stars are big and some are small. The Sun is a medium-sized star. It looks so big and bright because it is much closer to the Earth than any other star. The Sun and all the other stars swirl around in galaxies. Our galaxy is called the Milky Way Galaxy. When we look at the night sky, we see only a small number of the stars in our galaxy. It takes a big imagination to think about space.

The *Galileo* spacecraft took this photo of the Earth and Moon.

North Star Finder

For hundreds of years, the North Star has helped people find their way when they travel. When you see the North Star in the sky, you know you are facing north. The North Star is a very bright star near the Big Dipper. The Big Dipper looks like it turns around in a circle to face different directions at different times of the year.

Make a viewer to help you find the Big Dipper and North Star. As you look through the Star Finder, turn it in a circle to see how the pattern changes.

✔ star finder pattern   ✔ white glue

✔ tracing paper   ✔ clear tape (optional)

✔ pencil

✔ construction paper   ✔ pipe cleaner (optional)

✔ toilet tissue tube

✔ scissors

Let's Go!

1. Use tracing paper to trace the star finder pattern on page 27. Transfer the pattern from the tracing paper onto a piece of construction paper of any color.

2. Use a sharp pencil to poke holes in the dots on the star finder. Cut out the circle (See A).

3. Lay the cardboard tube on the construction paper and mark the length. Cut on the line.

Roll the construction paper around the tube so it overlaps. Glue or tape the strip of construction paper around the tube (See B). Let dry.

4. Glue the star finder circle to the end of the tube. If you wish, decorate the star finder with construction paper stars and pipe cleaner (See C).

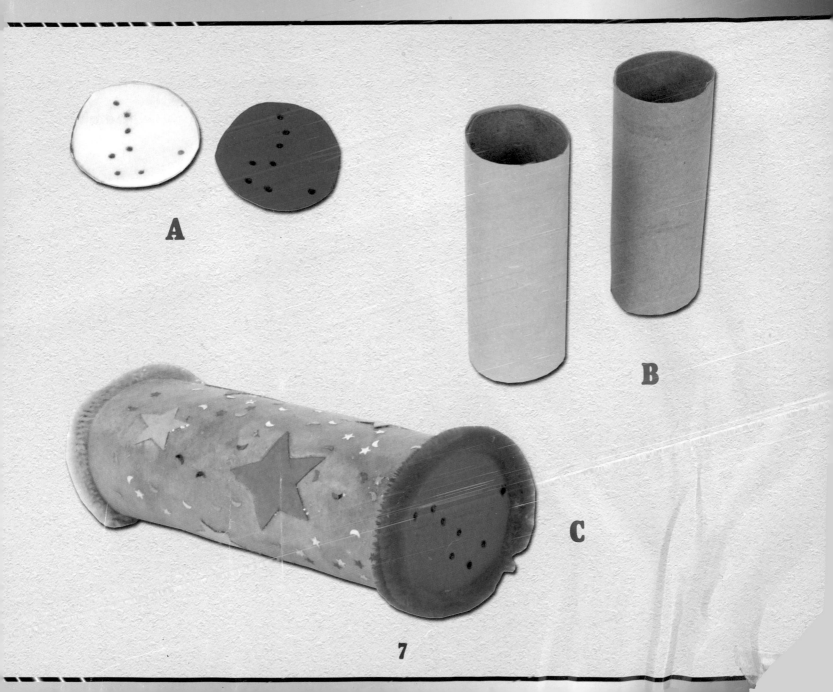

A

B

C

7

Phases of the Moon

An object that orbits around a planet is called a satellite. The Moon orbits around the Earth. The Moon is a natural satellite of planet Earth. Sometimes the Moon is between the Sun and the Earth. At these times, the Moon is lit from behind. The dark shadowed side of the Moon faces the Earth. The moon cannot be seen. This is the New Moon.

As the Moon travels around the Earth, different parts of it are lit by the Sun. We see the lit parts of the Moon from Earth. When the Earth is between the Sun and the Moon, the Moon is all lit up when seen from Earth. This is the Full Moon.

Get Set

- ✔ **9-inch paper plate**
- ✔ **paint**
- ✔ **white construction paper**
- ✔ **pencil**
- ✔ **crayons**
- ✔ **glitter (optional)**
- ✔ **scissors**
- ✔ **hole punch**
- ✔ **string**

Let's Go!

1. Use poster paint to paint both sides of a paper plate to look like the Sun. Paint one side of the paper plate (See A). Let dry. Paint the other side. Let dry.

2. On a piece of white construction paper, use a pencil to draw eight circles. (See page 28 for the pattern.) Use the chart on page 26 to color the moon phases with crayons or glitter. Each circle will be a different moon phase. Cut out the circles. On the back of each circle, write the name of the moon phase. Make sure each moon phase is facing the correct way and use a hole punch to make a hole in the top of each circle. Punch out eight evenly spaced holes around the paper plate (See B).

3. Cut nine pieces of string about 10 inches long. Set one piece aside. This will be used for the hanging loop.

4. Tie a piece of string to each of the moon phase circles (See C). Follow the moon phase chart and tie the other end of the string around the paper plate. To hang, tie the last piece of string through two opposite holes (See D).

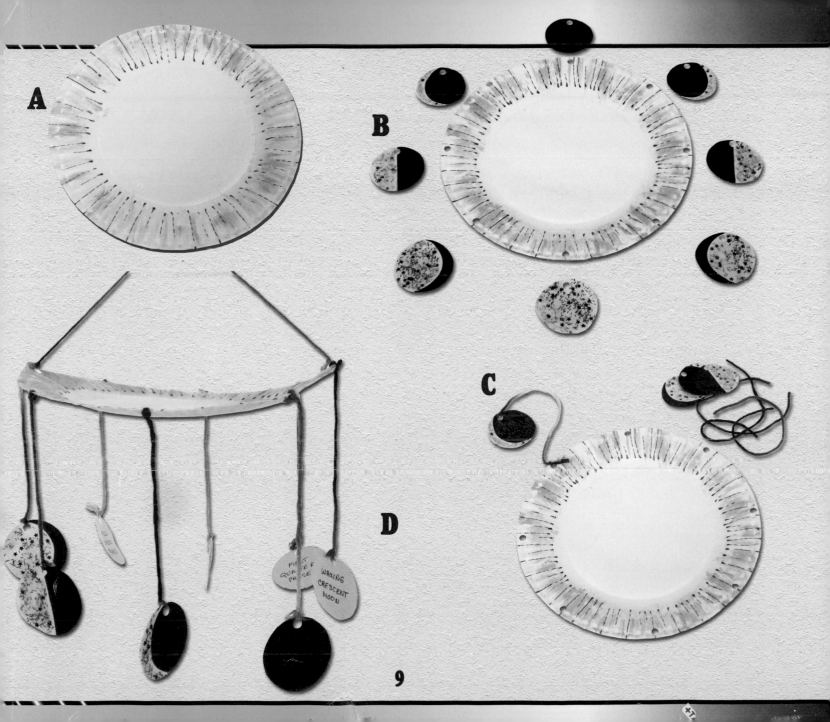

A

B

C

D

FIRST QUARTER PHASE

WAXING CRESCENT MOON

9

Space Shuttle Supply Holder

Are You Ready?

For many years, spaceships were built to last for only one trip into outer space. The space shuttle was the first spaceship built to go out into space and come back to Earth to be used again.

The space shuttle uses a big tank of rocket fuel and two rocket boosters to launch into space. These are used up and fall back to Earth within minutes after takeoff. The shuttle goes into orbit around the Earth. It holds a crew and supplies for them to live and work in space. Make a space shuttle to hold your supplies.

Get Set

- ✔ **paper towel tube**
- ✔ **cardboard from a cereal box**
- ✔ **pencil**
- ✔ **scissors**
- ✔ **clear tape**
- ✔ **newspaper**
- ✔ **white glue**
- ✔ **water**
- ✔ **paper bowl**
- ✔ **paintbrush**
- ✔ **poster paint**

Let's Go!

1. Lay the paper towel tube in the center of a piece of cardboard. Draw the winged shape of the space shuttle with the tube on top as the body of the shuttle (see page 28 for the pattern). Cut out the space shuttle shape and glue the tube down the middle of it. Let dry.

2. Cut out a cardboard circle to fit the bottom of the tube and glue it on. Let dry. If you wish, also use clear tape to hold the circle on to the tube.

10

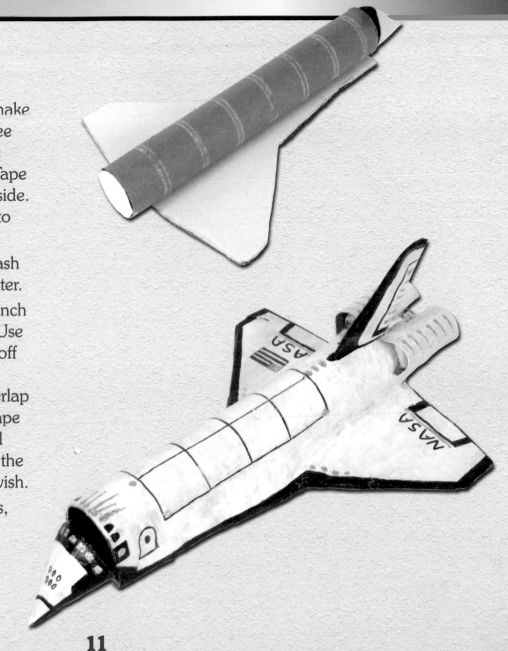

3. Cut out a larger half-circle and make a cone for the top of the tube (see page 28 for the pattern). Cut the cone to fit the top of the tube. Tape the cone on to the tube on one side. Tape the inside and the outside to make a hinge that opens.

4. In a paper bowl, make a glue wash using 2 parts glue and 1 part water.

5. Tear newspaper into 1-inch x 3-inch strips and dip in the glue wash. Use your fingers to slide excess glue off the newspaper strips. Cover the cardboard space shuttle and overlap the strips. Be sure to leave the tape hinge free of newspaper so it still opens and closes. Let dry. Paint the shuttle and add details, as you wish.

6. Keep your pens, pencils, brushes, and other cargo in the shuttle.

Space Glider

Are You Ready?

The space shuttle is a glider. It uses rockets to blast into space and small engines to move into orbit. But when the space shuttle returns to Earth, it uses gliding power to land. Its sleek body and broad wings help to keep it from falling fast to the Earth. Like a glider, it is launched from a height, and it uses its shape to lift it and hold it in the air.

The trick to making a really good paper glider is careful folding. The folds and creases should be sharp and both sides should be as even as possible. Use a ruler to make the creases very sharp. The launch is important, too. The glider should be level or pointed up.

Get Set

- ✔ **space glider diagram**
- ✔ **8½ x 11 computer paper**
- ✔ **ruler**
- ✔ **pencil**
- ✔ **markers (optional)**
- ✔ **crayons (optional)**
- ✔ **clear tape**

Let's Go!

1. Use the diagram on page 29 as a guide to make the space glider pattern. With a pencil and ruler, draw the lines onto a piece of computer paper (See A).
2. Fold along the center so the lines are on the outside. Open the paper.
3. Make a sharp crease on line 2. This will make a triangle (See B).
4. Fold on the center line so the lines are on the inside.
5. Fold along lines 3, 4, and 5. Pull the wings apart and gently push up the fold along line 2 (See C).
6. Tape the underside together at the place where you will hold the glider to launch it. If you wish, decorate the glider with markers or crayons (See D).
7. Hold the glider level and release it gently without jerking or spinning.

12

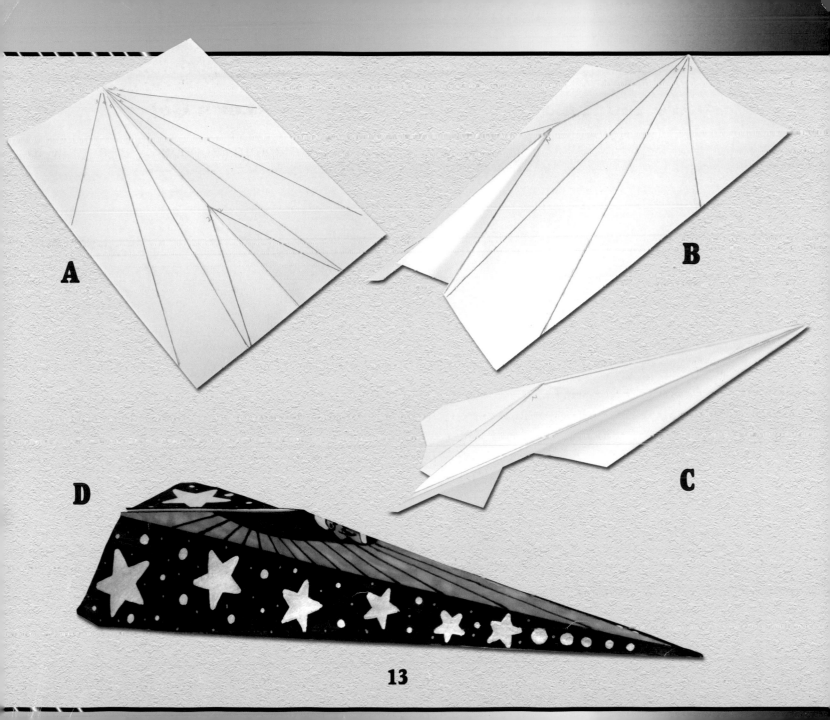

A

B

C

D

13

Space Colony

Space stations are large man-made satellites that humans can live in. The parts are taken into space by space shuttles and put together there by astronauts. Space colonies are future cities on other planets. Future space explorers who live in space colonies will need many of the same things space stations have. Build a model of a futuristic space city from recyclable materials and scraps.

Get Set

Ideas for Materials (Ask permission first!):

egg cartons, cardboard tubes, paper plates, drinking straws, toothpicks, plastic bubble packaging, wrapping paper, string, foil, construction paper, paper, fabric, buttons, cardboard

✔ **scissors**

✔ **white glue**

✔ **clear tape**

✔ **poster paint**

✔ **paintbrush**

Let's Go!

1. Collect scraps and materials (See A). Ask an adult to help you cut the materials you chose. Glue or tape them together to make interesting shapes. Look at pictures of satellites for inspiration.

2. Make round buildings, tube-shaped buildings, tall buildings with balconies, or short buildings with indoor gardens. Connect them with ramps, folded paper stairs, half-tubes, and slides (See B).

3. Decorate the space colony with colorful paper and poster paint (See C).

4. Make a city of the future, with far-out designs from your imagination!

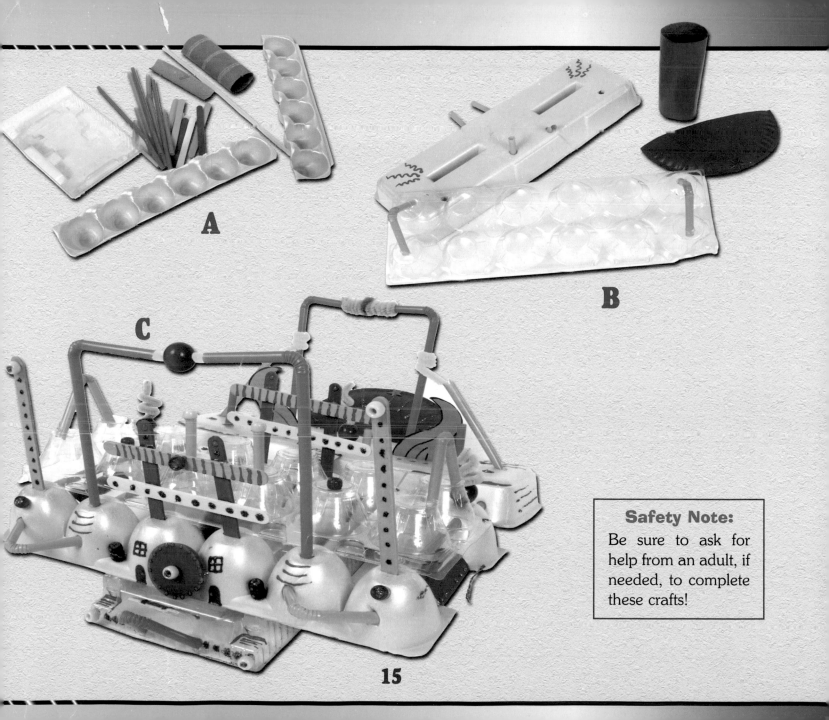

A

B

C

Safety Note:
Be sure to ask for
help from an adult, if
needed, to complete
these crafts!

15

My Favorite Planet

Planets circle around the Sun in our solar system. Mercury is the planet closest to the Sun. Earth is the third planet from the Sun, and the only one with liquid water. Saturn has big rings of ice particles circling around it. Which is your favorite planet? Make a model of your favorite planet from paper mâché.

Get Set

- ✔ balloon
- ✔ newspaper
- ✔ white glue
- ✔ water
- ✔ paper bowl
- ✔ brush
- ✔ scissors
- ✔ paper plate for rings (optional)
- ✔ paintbrush
- ✔ poster paint
- ✔ yarn (optional)
- ✔ masking tape (optional)

Let's Go!

1. To make a ringed planet, cut out the middle of a paper plate (See A). Blow up a balloon so it fits snugly inside the paper plate ring (See B). Tie off the balloon. Or use just a balloon alone for a planet with no rings.

2. In a paper bowl, make a glue wash using 2 parts glue and 1 part water.

3. Tear newspaper in small pieces, one inch or smaller. Separate the pieces and dip them in the glue wash. Use your fingers to slide excess glue off the newspaper pieces. Cover the balloon and paper plate with two layers of overlapping newspaper pieces. Let dry slightly.

If you would like to hang your planet, cut a piece of yarn about 24 inches. Use masking tape to secure about 2 inches of the yarn on the top of the balloon.

4. Continue covering the balloon and paper plate with newspaper placed in glue wash (See C). If you can see the color of the balloon through the newspaper, add more layers of newspaper. If it is too wet, add dry newspaper squares and brush them down. Let dry overnight. Look at pictures of your planet and paint it to match (See D). Let dry.

5. Try making the whole solar system!

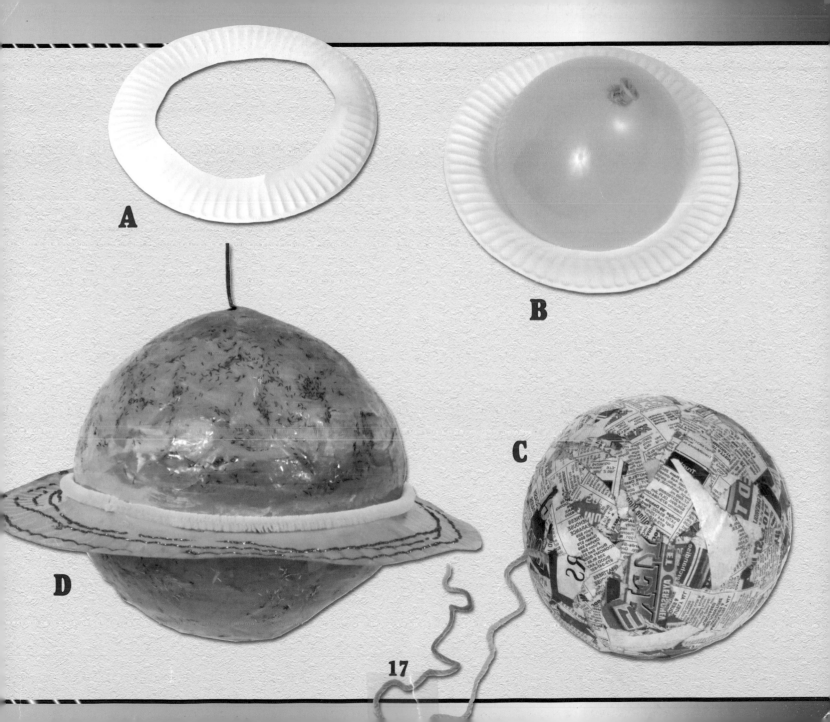

A

B

C

D

17

Earth Greetings

Are You Ready?

From Earth, the air we breathe in the sky full of clouds looks endless. But from outer space, our atmosphere looks like a thin blue shell. Earth looks like a shiny blue-green marble with white swirls. This is the view astronauts see from space shuttles.

Three-quarters of the Earth's surface is water, shining bright blue in the endless blackness of outer space. Clouds whirl around close to the surface, making changing patterns of white on the blue-green water planet. Make a greeting card showing what the Earth looks like from space.

Get Set

- ✔ black construction paper
- ✔ scissors
- ✔ white paper
- ✔ poster paint
- ✔ paintbrush
- ✔ white glue
- ✔ markers or pens

Let's Go!

1. Cut a piece of black construction paper and fold it in half to make a card.

2. On white paper, paint a picture of Earth as it looks from space. Make sure it will fit on the front of the card (see page 27 for the pattern). Cut it out.

3. Glue the Earth cutout to the front of the card. Let dry.

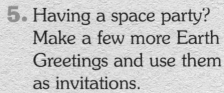

4. Cut a piece of white paper and glue it inside the card. Write a note to a friend on the white paper inside the card.

5. Having a space party? Make a few more Earth Greetings and use them as invitations.

Starry Night

Are You Ready?

Constellations are imaginary patterns of stars. They are pictures that help people find groups of stars in the sky. People make up constellations by drawing imaginary lines between stars. The Great Bear is a constellation near the North Pole. It contains the stars that form the Big Dipper. Make your own constellation.

Get Set

✔ **crayons**

✔ **watercolor paint**

✔ **paintbrush**

✔ **construction paper**

✔ **pencil**

Let's Go!

1. Decide on a picture. It could be a bear, a tree, or an apple. For a bear pattern, see page 29. It can be anything!

2. On a light-colored piece of construction paper, use a pencil to make dots in the shape of your design (See A). When you have it the way you want, use a crayon to go over the dots. Press down hard. Connect the dots to make your design.

Make other crayon dots all over the paper (See B). These are other stars.

3. Lightly brush dark-colored watercolor paint over the whole picture. The crayon will resist the watercolor and shine through (See C). Let dry.

4. What other constellations can you make?

20

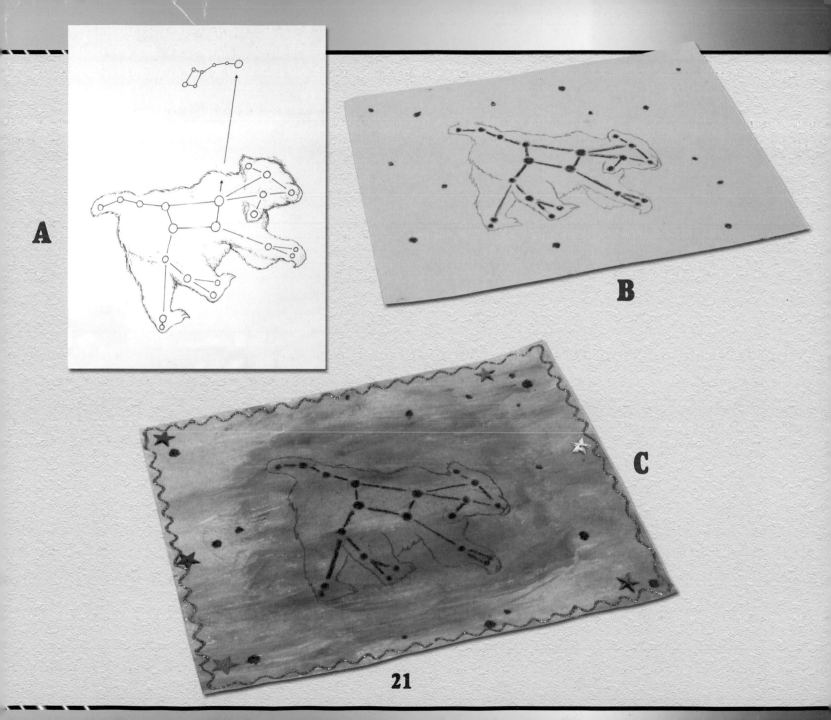

A

B

C

21

Comet's Tail

Comets are balls of ice, dust, and gas that loop around the sun. The sun burns off parts of the comet, creating long clouds that trail behind the comet. Comets look like stars with tails of light.

Make a comet picture frame with a long paper fringe.

Get Set

✔ **2 paper plates**

✔ **white glue**

✔ **clear tape (optional)**

✔ **4 sheets of white paper**

✔ **photograph (Ask permission first!)**

✔ **glitter**

✔ **scissors**

Let's Go!

1. Glue or tape four sheets of white paper together the long way to make a sheet about 43 inches long (See A).

2. Cut in a fringe. Glue the fringe on the side of the plate, on the back, so it hangs down like a comet tail. Let dry.

3. Glue a photograph in the center of the plate.

4. Cut a circle in the center of the second paper plate. Start with a small circle and put the plate over the picture to see how much to enlarge the hole (See B).

5. When the picture is framed just right, glue the edges of the plates together. Let dry. If you wish, decorate the frame with glitter (see C).

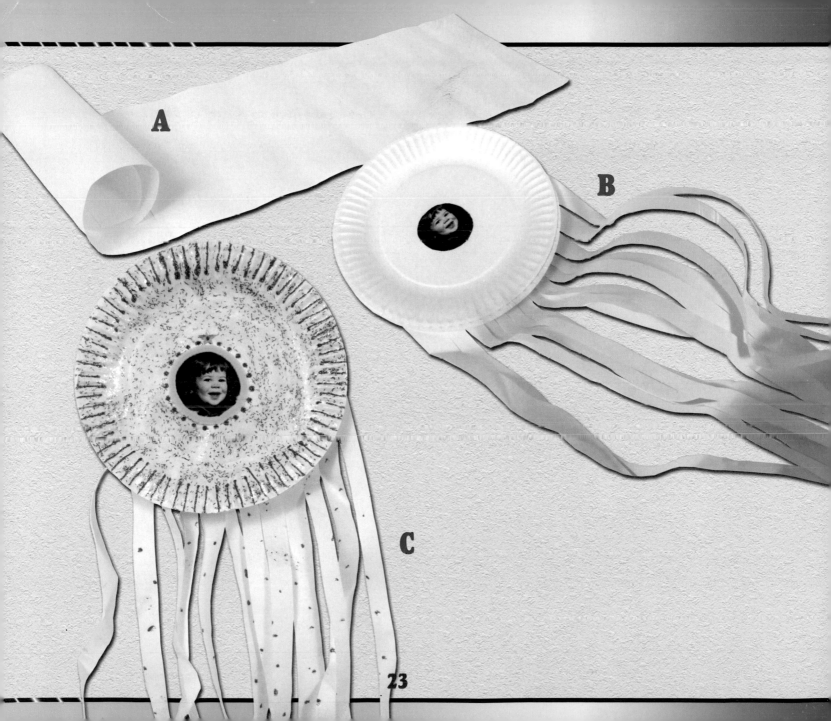

A

B

C

Flying Saucer

A UFO is an unidentified flying object. When someone sees something flying through space, and they do not know what it is, it is called a UFO. People have been seeing UFOs for thousands of years. They have been called by many names, including glowing discs, cloudships, spaceships, flying canoes, and flying saucers. UFOs are part of the mystery of space exploration.

Make a flying saucer that really flies.

Get Set

- ✔ 2 thick paper plates
- ✔ scissors
- ✔ plastic wrap
- ✔ paper or Styrofoam bowl
- ✔ clear tape
- ✔ 4 pennies
- ✔ white glue
- ✔ poster paint (optional)
- ✔ paintbrush (optional)

Let's Go!

1. Carefully cut out the center of two thick paper plates. You may also use two sets of two thin paper plates glued together (See A).

2. Place a paper or Styrofoam bowl, upside down, covering the hole in one paper plate. Glue the bowl down. Let dry.

3. Cover the top of the paper plate and bowl with one layer of plastic wrap. Tape the plastic wrap around the bottom of the paper plate. Slip the other cutout plate over the bowl so the plastic is sandwiched between the plates (See B).

4. Glue four pennies evenly spaced around the outside of the top paper plate. Let dry completely. If you wish, paint and decorate the flying saucer (See C). Let dry.

5. To launch the flying saucer, hold it level. To make it spin, flick your wrist as you let it fly.

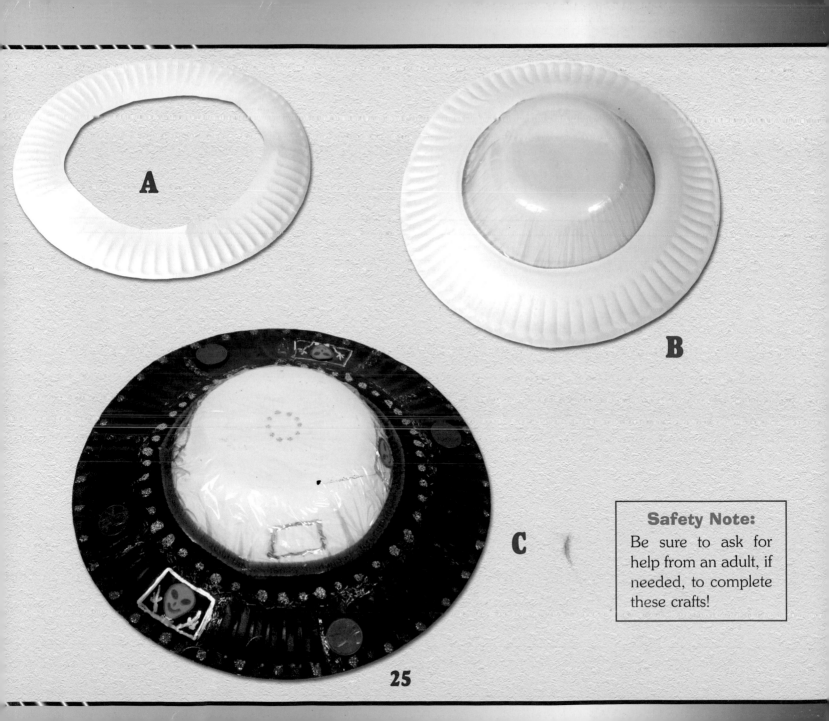

A

B

C

Safety Note:
Be sure to ask for help from an adult, if needed, to complete these crafts!

Moon Phase Chart

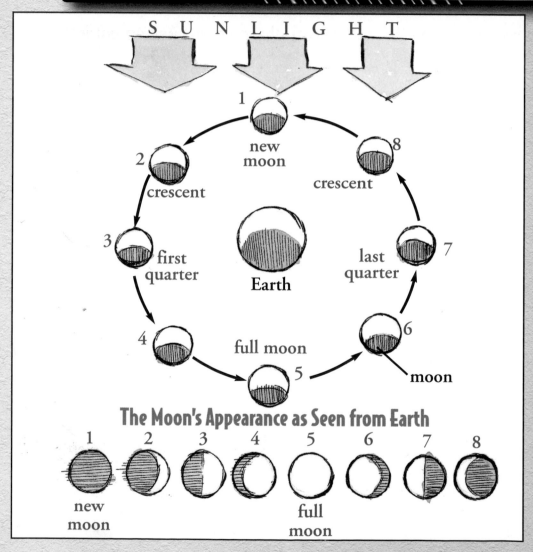

SUNLIGHT

1 new moon

2 crescent

3 first quarter

4

full moon 5

6 moon

7 last quarter

8 crescent

Earth

The Moon's Appearance as Seen from Earth

1 new moon

2

3

4

5 full moon

6

7

8

Use this chart to help you with the Phases of the Moon craft on page 8.

Patterns

Use tracing paper to copy the patterns on these pages. Ask an adult to help you cut and trace the shapes onto construction paper.

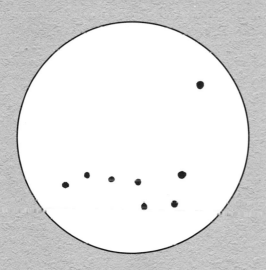

North Star Finder
Reduce to 1¾ inches

Earth Greetings
at 100%

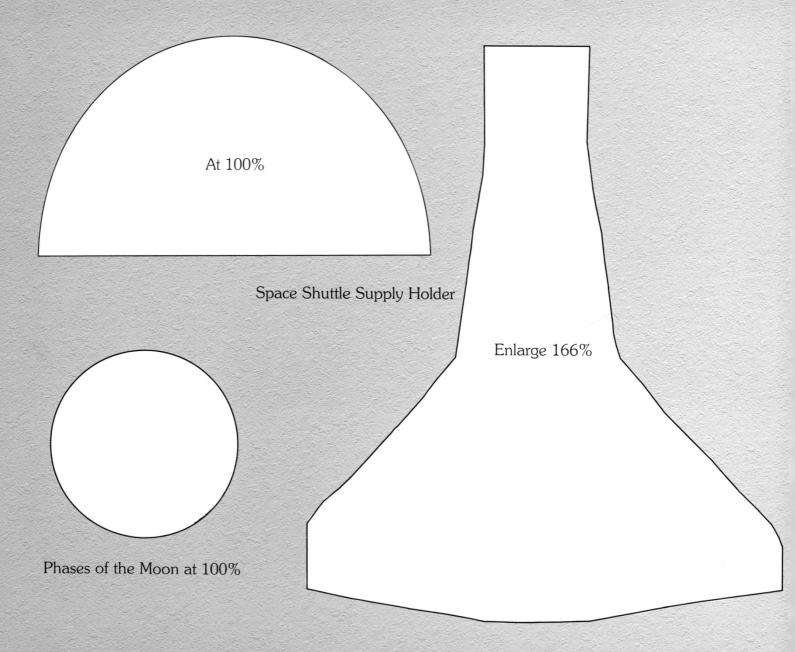

At 100%

Space Shuttle Supply Holder

Enlarge 166%

Phases of the Moon at 100%

28

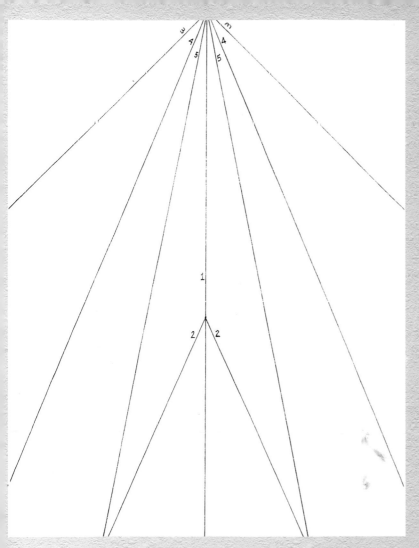

Space Glider
Enlarge 205%

Starry Night
Enlarge 221%

29

Reading About

Books

Bailey, Gerry. *Journey into Space*. Minneapolis, Minn.: Picture Window Books, 2005.

Gallant, Roy A. *The Planets*. New York: Benchmark Books, 2001.

Hans, E.M. *Constellations*. Austin, Tex.: Raintree Steck-Vaughn, 2001.

Nicolson, Cynthia Pratt. *Discover the Planets*. Toronto, Canada: Kids Can Press, 2005.

Nicolson, Cynthia Pratt. *Exploring Space*. Toronto, Canada: Kids Can Press, 2000.

Shearer, Deborah A. *Space Missions*. Mankato, Minn.: Bridgestone Books, 2003.

Internet Addresses

Solar System Exploration
<http://solarsystem.jpl.nasa.gov>
Check out the Kids section or learn more about the planets on this site from NASA.

Virtual Solar System
<http://www.nationalgeographic.com/solarsystem/splash.
    html>
Learn more about the solar system.

Index